# DARK PSYCHOLOGY SECRETS

*Mental Manipulation, persuasion techniques, and mind control methods. Learn How to Win Friends and Influence People. A step by step guide.*

BENEDICT SPOT
&
RICHARD EMPATH

# TABLE OF CONTENTS

# INTRODUCTION

Every time dark psychology comes up, we always think of mind control, persuasion, and manipulation. Generally speaking, we tend to believe that some evil art is practiced for the sake of advancing some malicious agenda. Other times, most individuals believe that we are talking about some type of magic spells that are cast on the minds of people.

The fact of the matter that dark psychology derives its name from the fact that it deals with the ways in which individuals, organizations and even governments can use mental triggers to sway people's opinions one way or another.

For instance, governments tend to highly publicize their achievements in order to convince voters that they are doing a good job. This is quite common when incumbents are up to for reelection or are looking to further their foothold.

Skeptics like to point out how religions and advertisers use dark psychology, through mental manipulation, to essentially brainwash people to go along with their agendas. The fact is that "brainwashing" as is generally portrayed in Hollywood films that quite work that way. That is, when you think about manipulation, it isn't about a group of thugs beating people and force-feeding them content so that victims and easily control-lable.

In reality, mental manipulation is a very subtle art. When done properly, subjects don't even know they are being manipulated. As a matter of fact, they are perfectly happy to go along with the manipulators' agenda.

Consider this example: Advertisers often use scare tac-tics to persuade you to purchase an item. They will generally present you with a problem, which is usually life-altering (though it generally isn't), and then with a solution. The solution is the product or service which they sell. Then, they load up on the consequences that come with not acquiring their solution. So, if you don't buy their product, you will suffer grave consequences.

A common example is health. A great deal of products in the health industry are aimed at weight loss. So, advertisers claim that if you are overweight you are prone to any number of health risks. While the science backs that up, they blow those claims out of proportion. This leads folks to begin to question their health. Then, the advertiser will present their product as the ultimate weight-loss solution. Finally, you will be a healthy individual because you have lost weight thanks to their product.

While all of that may actually be true, some advertisers go over the top by including bogus science, false testimonials and actors posing as doctors. Some of the more gullible viewers fall for the advertising and purchase the product(s). The products' ultimate effectiveness is then up to the user's own experience.

In this book, we will be taking a look at how you can learn how dark psychology works so that you can not only recognize when such techniques are being used on you. This will help you vastly improve your personal relationships while helping you get ahead in all facets of your life. So, whether you are brand new to this subject or whether you have learned about it in the past, this volume will certainly provide you with fresh insights and perspective on how dark psychology is used in everyday life.

## Chapter 1

# WHAT IS MENTAL MANIPULATION

The term "mental manipulation" is often thrown around on social media and in mainstream communications. In fact, it is quite common to hear this expression used in reference to large public events, political campaigning and advertising. The fact of the matter is that most folks have a general understanding of what it refers to but may not be clear on the specific of what this term encompasses.

In short, mental manipulation is controlling and twisting a person's state of mind to make them want to do what you want to be done. A manipulator influences the will of others through the use deception or underhand techniques.

As such, manipulation implies a degree of force upon targets, that is, the manipulator will try their best to force their targets to do what they will, especially if the targets do not wish to comply.

Now, I am not talking about kidnapping folks and brainwashing them like it is done in the movies. I am talking about subtle techniques and strategies which are used to get others to go along without them actually realizing they are being manipulated.

As a matter of fact, the best manipulators make it seem like people are doing things of their own accord rather than acting upon the provocation of some external force. Nevertheless, there is a degree of forces that goes along with manipulation. For example, television stations will force you to watch their programming and advertising in order to get you to purchase the products and services of their sponsor's.

However, the coercion shown in this case is quite simple to get around: you can just change the channel. Yet, programming and advertising is designed in such a way that you won't want to change channel.

Other types of manipulation can be a lot more overt. For instance, political parties and candidates will promote themselves by littering their campaigns with calls to action such as "vote for the best candidate" or "vote for so-and-so if you value your children's future". These calls to action are blatant attempts at swaying voters' opinions.

That is why the first part of this book is dedicated to understanding and identifying manipulation as it is commonly practiced. I am not talking about some dark cabal that is trying to secretly rule the world through controlling the minds of every single human on this planet. In fact, I am referring to the ways in which trained individuals will attempt to influence your opinion to get you to go along with their agenda.

When you uncover their techniques, you will not only be able to protect yourself, and your loved ones, from these influences, you will be also be able to get your own agenda across. While I am not asking you to openly go out there and control the minds of those with whom you come into contact, I am asking you to use these techniques to help you get ahead when you need that extra nudge.

So, sit back because we are going on quite a ride.

*Chapter* 2

# WHAT IS DARK PSYCHOLOGY

Dark psychology is the art of using manipulation and mind control over others. It is the study of human conditions about how people prey on others. We all have the potential to oppress other human beings and creatures. Most of us restrain this feeling, but some utilize it. Dark psychology tries to find out the perceptions, behaviors, and thoughts that lead to this preying behavior. In most cases, dark psychology has found that 99.99% is goal-oriented, and the remaining 0.01% manipulate others with no purpose and with no influence from religious dogma and science. Therefore, dark psychology is the trend in which people use techniques like persuasion, manipulation, and motivation to get their way. What is a dark psychology triad?

Dark psychology triad is the seeking to foretell the criminal behavior and manipulation in relationships. These triads are narcissism, which is the grandiosity, egotism, and lacking empathy, psychopathy, which is using charm and friendliness, but lacking empathy, selfishness, and remorsefulness to get what you want and Machiavellianism, which is manipulating others with deception and lacking morality in your manipulation. Nobody wants to be manipulated, but in today's world, we are prone to be manipulated. It does not have to be in extreme cases like the dark triad above, but we are manipulated in simple actions that may seem harmless and normal. You will find this manipulation in sales techniques, in the internet ads, and our children when they seek to get what they want. People we love and trust a lot apply dark psychology to us.

Dark psychology involves everything that human beings are in their dark part. We all have a masked side within us from birth that is evil. Dark psychology has found out that these people who do these acts never do it for sex, power, retribution, or any other purpose. They commit these heinous acts with no goal in mind. They violate and harm others just for the thrill of it.

Like I mentioned, we all have that potential in us. The potential to harm others without explanation or reason. Dark psychology takes this potential to be difficult and complex to explain. Let us look at the 0.01% manipulators in dark psychology.

**Predator** - This is a person or persons who exploit, victimize, stalk, or coerce others using information in technology. They have desires and fantasies to control and get power. Predators can be of any age and gender who indulge in cyberstalker, cyberbully, internet troll, cyber-terrorist, online psychopath, or who engages in internet defamations.

**Arsonist** - This is a person who is obsessed with fire and its settings. These types of people have a history of physical and sexual abuse. Most arsonists are loners, have few peers, and are impressed by fire. They are ritualistic and set fires on a pattern. They get their targets and set it ablaze to get sexual arousal and feel proud.

**Necrophilia** - These are people with disorders and have a sexual attraction to dead people. They have a problem and get sexually attracted to things or corpses.

## Chapter 3

# HISTORICAL OUTLINE OF MENTAL MANIPULATION

Every tree with sweet fruits hanging on its strong branches stemmed from a seed. Funny enough, even the trees with poisonous fruits came from tiny seedlings; they did not fall from the sky. Let us dig the ground together and understand where this villain called mental manipulation stemmed from. The birth of mental manipulation has to begin with the study by Jonathan Edwards, who discovered it in the 18th Century. It was during a crusade in Massachusetts when he discovered it accidentally. He found that by making Christians feel guilty and increasing the tension on them, they would always attend the meetings and submit completely. Charles J. Finney also used this mental manipulation for four years in his ministry, and even today, many revivalists are using it on their Christians. As a result of the mental manipulation, one person attempted to take his life, and another committed suicide. Most people confessed that they were also affected and always had suicidal feelings pushing them. Most preachers still manipulate their followers mentally intending to increase their followings especially the televised variety. Mental manipulation was first formulated on Christians, but scientists have also used it in the past.

## BRAIN PHASES

Pavlov, a Russian scientist, identified the states in which our brain responds to stimuli. The equivalent was the first phase, where our mind reacted the same to strong and weak stimuli. Paradoxical was the next phase where the mind favored weak stimuli than strong stimuli. Ultra-paradoxical is the last phase the brain adapts to conditioning. It turns positive behavior to negative and vice versa when conditioned. As you continue to manipulate the person mentally, the person becomes controlled. There are so many ways to manipulate a person mentally, but it mostly occurs in religion and politics. The first step is to work on a person's emotions until they are in complete anger, excitement, fear or tension. Mental manipulation intends to increase suggestibility and impair your judgment. When this manipulation is maintained, it compounds. Once the first stage is implemented, the manipulator has total control over the victim's brain, and he or she can replace the former mental programming with new patterns of his or her choice.

There are also more psychological weapons used to manipulate your mental capacities such as physical discomfort, fasting, mantra chanting as used in meditation, special lighting, intoxicating drugs, and sound effects, among many others. When these methods are used to manipulate you, they get the same outcome like in psychiatric treatment using the shock treatment or lowering a person's insulin with injection. Mental manipulation is different from hypnosis- mental manipulation is far stronger. However, you can mix the two and get powerful results.

Even after many years have passed since it was discovered, our politicians, lawyers, and different people in society are using mental manipulation in our churches. Most of them do it with a goal in mind. They will communicate with a soft, patterned and well-paced voice to control your mind.

*Chapter 4*

# TECHNIQUES USED IN MENTAL MANIPULATION

## PERSUASION TECHNIQUE

Persuasion is controlling the human mind without the knowledge of the manipulated party. The manipulated party will change his or her opinion without being aware. This technique accesses your right mind, which is imaginative and creative, while the left side is rational and analytical. In persuasion, the perpetrator distracts your left brain and occupy it. It leaves you in an eyes-open altered state but still conscious, making you move from Beta awareness to Alpha. This technique is famous for politicians and lawyers.

## SUBLIMINAL PROGRAMMING

These are masked suggestions that can only be understood by your subconscious mind. They can be suggestions in audios, airbrushed visual suggestions, and flash images on your television quickly so that you do not consciously notice them. Some subliminal programming on audio makes suggestions on low volume. Your subconscious mind will notice these suggestions, but no one can monitor them even with equipment. The music we listen to can have a second voice behind it to program your mind. In 1984, a newsletter called Brain-Mind Bulletin that 99% of our activities are non-conscious.

**Mass misuse** - During mass meetings, the attendees go in and out of consciousness. If you have no idea, you cannot notice what is happening to you. It is a mental manipulation of the mass through vibrations. These vibrations produce Alpha, which makes the mass vulnerable. These make them accept any suggestion of the speaker as a command.

**Vibrato** - Vibrato is some effect installed on instrumental music or vocal, which makes people go in a distorted state of mind. In English history, some singers who had vibrato in their voices were not given chances to perform because of the effect they had on the public. Some listeners would have fantasies, mostly sexual fantasies.

**Neurophone** - Dr. Patrick Flanagan invented Neurophone. It is a device that can program your mind when it gets in contact with your skin. When this device gets in contact with your skin, you lose your sense and sight for a moment. It is because the skin has sensors for pain, touch, vibration, and heat. The message to manipulate your mind is played through Neurophone, which is connected and placed in the ceiling and no speakers. This message goes directly to the brain of the audience, and the manipulator can easily manipulate their mental state.

**Medium for take-over** - When you know how human beings function, you get the ability to control them. Medium take-over is happening in the televisions we watch. When people are put in a distorted state of mind, they function on the right brain, which releases brain opiates and makes you feel good, and you want it more. The experience is the same as the one opium users feel. The broadcasts in our televisions induce the

Alpha making us accept the broadcast easily. It makes viewers translate suggestions as commands. Every minute spent on watching television conditions us.

*Chapter 5*

# WHAT ARE THE SIGNS OF MANIPULATION AS IT IS USED IN TODAY IN THE WORLD (PRACTICAL EXAMPLES)

Manipulation happens in all kinds of relationships in our society. It happens between lovers, between pastors and their following, and politicians manipulate us as well, among many other relationships. In this chapter, we will look at the signs of manipulation in different relationships.

## CHURCHES

Manipulation in the church can occur in both ways. The people in the church leadership can manipulate their followers and vice versa. It is sad since most of us look at the church as the source of your peace. Most of us go for spiritual nourishment when we feel down from the church. How sad can it be if the church can be the source of your pain? Let us look at how the pastors can manipulate their followers.

## 1. Lack of open and honest conversations

In some churches, you are not allowed to ask questions. If you find yourself in such a situation, you are met with excuses or dismissal on not getting the information. It is okay when there are concerns not to divulge information that will interfere with the privacy of other members. The leaders should take responsibility for their actions and always be ready to explain to the members why there are certain rules. Church information should be open to its members, and there should be transparency.

## 2. Leaders never admit their mistakes

We can forgive our pastors for making mistakes. After all, they are human beings, but it is difficult to forgive them when they fail to communicate. Yes, I know what the Bible says about forgiveness, but remember, I am a human being too. When leaders refuse to admit to their mistakes and are always spinning their actions to fit those of a perfect lamb of God, they create a difficult situation. You should watch out for some recurring defensiveness in your church's leadership. You should also watch out if the church is masking some of its mistakes.

## 3. They use shame as an influence mechanism

Some churches in our community use shame to influence their members. They will shame their members for giving little money, shame them for missing the service and shame them for their actions. Even with no knowledge of the world, the Bible is clear that to those who belong to Christ, there is no condemnation. Remember, none of those in the church leadership will sit on the judgment seat at the end of the world. Some of them act as if they have the final say on who will enter the gates of heaven. They will use the carrot and stick theory to manipulate you.

## 4. They are selective

First of all, you should understand that God created us all equally, and He accepts us the way we are. In some churches, they will restrict you to dress in a certain manner, they will choose people of a certain color, and they will force their members to follow some stipulated rules for them to fellowship in that church. The church should not have superficial lines but should be an all-inclusive place. The church should emulate Christ, who embraced all the rich such as Lazarus and the prostitutes, such as Mary Magdalene. Do not get me wrong; rules and regulations are important to run any organization but rules created to exclude a certain group of people in the wrong. Church leaders should know that they are servants.

Now I do not want you to think that pastors are evil for such actions above. You might find that some are not even aware of these manipulative actions, but others do it intentionally. Flipping the coin, pastors are also prone to manipulation. The church members can do it without the pastors realizing it. All the same, neither of the manipulations is acceptable. Let us look at the other side of the coin and find out how the church members can manipulate their pastors.

## Compliments

Compliments are good as they encourage us and make us feel good. Now some members may use compliments to manipulate you. They will seek to influence your decisions in the church's agenda through flattery. You should watch out for such signs, as they are as bad as using criticism to bully another.

## Criticisms

Well, you can never avoid criticism, especially if you have a leadership role. During conversations, some members will criticize your actions using their tone and sometimes body language. Always follow the church's rules and regulations and the teachings of the Bible. Be gentle when responding to such scenarios, and you will settle the manner amicably.

## Silence

They tell us that silence is the best tool to silence manipulation, but it can also be a sign of manipulation. You find members giving you the silent treatment to control you. The pastor should be aware of this and should not carry the burden but instead should pray for the members.

## Prayers

Pastors should take caution with the people they share with their burdens. They should protect themselves and their families from over-exposure. They should find trusted friends to share with their challenges, and even then, they should choose what is important to share and what is not.

## FAMILIES

As we mentioned, earlier, manipulation happens in all kinds of relationships. It can be intentionally used or unintentionally, but in the end, the other party ends up doing something they did not want to do in the first place. In our homes, parents can manipulate their children, and the children can manipulate their parents as well. Children learn at an early age that they can get what they want through tantrums and when you give in, they get control. Away from the children. Now, what are the signs that teens are manipulating their caregivers?

## 1. Steamrolling

Teenagers make endless and repetitive requests that are meant to wear out the caregivers to get their way. They will use the 'can I' 'how about now' language all the time. The act like a broken record that keeps playing the same song repeatedly.

## 2. Lying

Teenagers love to tell little white lies or omitting some parts of the truth to get what they want. They leave out some details if given, would change your affirmation to their request. Most of them also collaborate on the small lies in case the parents communicate; they will have the same information and allow them their request.

## 3. Retaliation

Most teenagers do some hurtful things to retaliate for not getting their way. They will not clean their room; they will dress inappropriately, they will put on loud music; all these as an attempt to get even with you. It is difficult because you cannot yell at them to stop since they are no longer children, and most caregivers end up giving in to their demands to avoid these hurtful actions.

Caregivers can as well manipulate their children, and it is bad since the children are in their developing age, and it makes their life difficult. Briefly, let us look at the signs that a caregiver is manipulating the child.

- They do not give the child security and affirmation
- They are always critical.
- The caregiver always demands the attention of the child.
- The caregiver makes toxic jokes about the child.
- The caregiver does not allow the child to express their negative emotions
- The caregiver scares the child.

## POLITICS

Politicians engage the emotional system of your brains to get political mileage. They use fear, disgust, and anger and never compassion or hope. Politicians never inspire us to work together for the common good of us all. They use anger, fear, and disgust to manipulate how we vote. They influence how we feel about other candidates and their policies. Most of us are never aware that we are being manipulated.

## 1. Informing you that the turn-out will be high

Politicians will tell you that they turn out will be high to motivate you to go to the polls. If they told you that the turn out would be low, most would not turn out since it depresses the efforts to go out and vote.

## 2. Public shaming

The politicians will never shame you publicly to safe-guard their reputation and their votes, but they can use other means to make you feel bad for not voting. You would get ads and letters asking you what your relatives and friends would think of you if you did not vote. It will push you to vote.

## 3. Making promises or threats to follow up with you

It is natural for human beings to do things in the right way when their actions are under observation. In the 2010 US election, some people received a letter to encourage them to vote. Others received the same letter, but with an addition that they will be called to share their voting experience. It brought more voter turnout than the previous general election.

*Chapter 6*

# HOW TO RECOGNIZE A MANIPULATOR AND WHAT ARE THE SIGNS OF MANIPULATION (ADD A LOT OF DETAILS)

Each one of us has been manipulated in one way or the other. Some of us have been manipulated for many years without understanding that they are being manipulated. Recognizing a manipulator is hard since they manipulate you in secret. Manipulators are unscrupulous, skillful, and self-centered. They never leave behind fingerprints when they commit this crime, but the good thing is we can understand and predict this behavior if we know what we are looking for. How can you recognize a manipulator?

## MANIPULATORS UNDERMINE YOUR CONVICTION TO GRASP THE REALITY

Manipulators are good at lying. They can insist that an episode happened, but it didn't, or they insist that it did happen, but in reality, it didn't happen. I know it sounds easy to escape such a trap, but they are so good at this tactic that they will make you question your sanity.

## THEIR ACTIONS AND WORDS ARE DISSIMILAR

Manipulators have a way with words. They will always tell you what will tick you, but their actions go in the opposite direction. They will promise to change, they will promise to support you, but when it comes to implementing their promises, they will act as if you are asking for a lot from them. They will insist on how blessed and lucky they are to have you in their life, but their actions will portray that you are a burden to them. You should be keen on this behavior because it also undermines your grasp of reality.

## THEY ARE GOOD AT A GUILT-TRIPPING THEIR VICTIMS

Have you ever met someone who made a mistake, but instead of owning up to their mistake, they made you feel guilty for their mistakes? Manipulators have mastered this art, and they will never allow you to complain of their wrong actions because when you do, they make you feel bad for bringing it up, and in cases where you keep it to yourself, they also make you feel bad for not bringing it up. In some cases, they will make you feel sorry for them by acting as the victim, yet they are on the wrong. They will use a tone of desperation or sometimes result in silent treatment to make you feel guilty for something bad they did.

## THEY HAVE AN APPETITE FOR POWER

They have an arrogant attitude that makes them believe that they are superior to everyone else. They use this sense of superiority to control you and feel a sense of power. Their appetite for power is insatiable.

## DOES HE OR SHE RAISE HIS OR HER VOICE?

Manipulators have a misplaced sense of power and always feel entitled to everything. When things don't go as they had planned, they may result in raising their act, voice, or become aggressive. They do that to coerce you to agree with their plans or idea.

## THEY USE NEGATIVE JOKES TO HURT YOU

Manipulators will make fun of your looks, your cooking, and your mode of communication in a masked manner to hide their real intentions. They do this to show superiority over you.

## SWEET-TALKING

I know we all love to hear sweet words about ourselves and our deeds, but this is a different kind of sweet-talking. Manipulators' sweet talks have no truth in it. They use it to deceive you. We relate to people differently. For instance, the way you relate with your best friend is different from the way you relate with a stranger. Manipulators hasten connections by using sweet talks. At the same time, if you are observant, you will notice that their actions and sweet words do not match.

## THEY TAKE ADVANTAGE OF ALL WEAK SPOTS

Manipulators are smart people and are aware of your weak spot through observation or talking you into divulging that information. They know all your insecurities and never hesitate to use them against you. They use that information to manipulate you instead of reassuring you and making you feel better.

## THEY ALWAYS HAVE IT WORSE THAN YOU DO

We all have problems and difficult situations in this life. In a situation where you are sharing a problem with a manipulator, they never listen and make you feel better. They always have a worse problem than yours up their sleeve. They will make you feel bad for complaining because your problem does not legit to complain about.

## THEY USE CHARM AND NICENESS

Manipulators may use charm to get sex or power. They do not struggle to use charm; it comes naturally to them. Their conscious does not limit them to use it to hurt others. In most cases, they are good at studying your behavior, and with time, they get to know your needs. They then give you what you needed to have you coiled in their little thumb.

## THEY ARE FOND OF DENYING

Manipulators never admit their mistakes. If they wrong you and you bring it to their attention, they deny it. They never take responsibility for their mistakes or bad behaviors.

## THEY USE LIES AS A WEAPON

They have no problem with lying, as their conscience is impaired. They never miss a chance to get anything they need; instead, they use lies to get it. They lie by withholding information or distorting the truth.

## GENEROSITY WITH GIFTS

Some manipulators can be kind and generous. I know it sounds unbelievable, but you should already guess that they do so with an intent. They will shower you with gifts and give you favors to get bigger favors from you shortly. You might think that these acts are their way of expressing love, but if you pay attention to their character, you will find out otherwise.

## THEY USE COMPLIMENTS IN EXCESS

Manipulators will shower you with compliments in excess. They will flatter you at every opportunity. Compliments are good, and they make us feel good about ourselves, but when you notice they are too much, it is important to ask yourself what that person wants from you.

## FORCED TEAMING

Manipulators will act like you are in the same team to create a notion of unity and togetherness with their victims. They will often use the word we, but instead of you feeling comfortable with it, you will feel discomfort, and you will not have the will to refuse because you will appear rude.

## SIGNS OF MANIPULATION

We already know how you can recognize a manipulator, but how can you tell if you are being manipulated? Let us find out the signs of manipulation.

## HOME COURT ADVANTAGE

As we already know, manipulation is all about control. Manipulators take you away from familiar grounds to unfamiliar ones to have an advantage over gaining control over you. A manipulator will take you on a date at his favorite restaurant, make you hang out with his friends. They do that to feel in control because it is easy to control a person who is not comfortable with the surroundings.

## PLAIN OLD BULLYING

A manipulator will bully you with his or her actions to do something. They will make a request, but their tone of voice and body language indicates a threat in case you fail to do it. Once you do what they had requested, they will tell you that you did not have to do it and make you look like you had a choice, and you did not.

## TUGGING ON YOUR HEARTSTRINGS

A manipulator will make you feel bad for saying no. In normal situations, people come to common ground when making a decision, and it is acceptable if you are not comfortable with some ideas, but in manipulation, you have no right to say no because when you do, the manipulator will make you feel like you are the worst person on earth.

## EMOTIONAL BLACKMAIL

In manipulation, the manipulators will make you do stuff for them with a condition. For instance, your boyfriend might ask you to visit his aging grandma, and when you refuse because of different reasons, they can threaten to harm themselves.

## PLAYING THE VICTIM

In manipulation, the perpetrator does something wrong but acts like the victim. They will make you apologize for their mistakes. The manipulator is always helpless and hurt, and this makes you feel like you are the bad one in the relationship. They make their victims feel bad, and at the same time, they avoid being accountable for their mistakes.

## GASLIGHTING

Gaslighting is a manipulation tactic that makes you feel like you are going mad. The manipulator will say ugly things to you and then pretend that they didn't; they will twist information, pretend like they did not say some of it, leave out some vital information and make you think you are going dander. When they apply this technique for a long time, you feel as if you cannot trust yourself and your thinking. You stop relying on your judgment to make decisions and start relying on theirs.

## Chapter 7

# HOW TO DEFEND YOURSELF FROM THOSE WHO WANT TO MANIPULATE US

Manipulative people tend to disguise their interests as one`s interests. In other words, they are the kind of people who will believe that their opinions, as well as facts, are the best and yours doesn't count. They will attract any form of attention and take credit in places where they don't deserve it. They are the kind of people who will tell everyone how incompetent you are. They will then work on improving your skills so as they can use you to get more credit. If you fail to change the way they want, they will ruin your life. It is worth noting that they are the kind of people who will help you so as they can control you as well. In other words, they will force you to change not to better your life but so as they can use you. They will do all they can to ensure that they will keep you from outgoing them. They can't allow you to outshine them although they will pretend to be helping you. It is worth noting that once you enable manipulative people in your life, they are tough to get rid of. In other words, they will flip flop issues and make your success path to be slippery and confusing. They are the kind of people who will ensure that they have used all your efforts for their benefits. Thus, it is wise to avoid them and get rid of their schemes and plans. Take a look at some of the techniques you can use to prevent their projects.

## IGNORE EVERYTHING THEY DO AND SAY

When you are dealing with manipulative people, one of the biggest mistakes you can do is correct them. In other words, a manipulative person thinks that his way of doing things in the best, and there is no way it can be changed. They have their tactics that they believe they are the best and all the other people under their custody can`t have better ideas than they do. In other words, the art of correcting them should be the aspect you need to avoid. However, what you need to do is to ignore everything they do or say. Also, you should work hard and ensure that they don`t realize or understand the things that trigger you most. The aspect is linked to the fact that once they have known the things that trigger you, they will use them to influence all your actions. Uniquely if they can identify the things you love most, they will use them as a bait to manipulate or somewhat control all your activities. One of the best strategies to avoid the manipulative aspect is to ignore their ideas. What you need to do is to delete all their ideas in your minds. Don't show concerned with what they want you to do? The aspect is linked to the fact that they will ensure that they have corned you and ensure that they have the credit they want from you. If they happen to be your relatives or your bosses, you may agree with what they say but turn around and do your things. At first, they will be pissed off by your actions and end up ignoring you once they realize that you aren't interested in what they believe. However, if you will accidentally do what they like doing, they will end up manipulating you.

## HIT THEIR CENTER OF GRAVITY

It is worth noting that manipulative people will always use their strategies to ensure that they are against you. For instance, they may hold past actions over your head and tell your friends to turn against you. They are the kind of people who will become your friends to your loved ones so as they can sue them to ill-treat you. They may even get a step further to reward your friends and ensure that they all turn against you. At such moments, they will then pretend to be good friends so as you can tell them all your secrets. They will, in turn, utilize such secrets to ensure that they have controlled all your actions. The aspect is linked to the fact that if they identify your past mistakes as well as the things you won't like to know by others, you will probably do whatever they ask so as they can instill the secret. The best thing for you to do is to turn the tables and ensure that the deals you have with them turn out to be miserable. If you have an experience with them, you can ignore all their attempts of be-friending you and close all the lope holes where they can understand about your secrets. The aspect is linked to the fact that they will lack a chance of manipulating you. You need to find their center of gravity. In other words, you need to identify the things that cause havoc in them. Pinpoint their strengths and work on reducing them to ashes. In other words, if they use words to convince people, ensure that you didn't offer any listening ear to them. Some use parties to influence their victims. Thus, you need to avoid such parties or any offers they give to people so as they can win. Some may have a deeper understanding of a particular aspect of life. Maybe it is a specific resource they control. What you need to do is to avoid all their strategies and ensure that you didn't close their paths. The aspect is critical in the sense that you will be in a good position of avoiding the things that could escalate their manipulative elements in your life.

## TRUST THE JUDGMENTS YOU MAKE

What you need to understand is that you are the best and whatever decision you are about to make is yours, and no one can do the best as you do. The aspect is critical in the sense that you will be in a good position avoiding the art of being manipulated. In other words, you will avoid cases where someone is using your capabilities to explore your emotions as well as the things you like. You need to define your life and trust your decisions. You don't have to get approval from people so as you can move on with what you think will work out the best for you. You need to understand that your boundaries are your beliefs. In other words, you need to set your limits and stick to them. The aspect is critical in the sense that it helps an individual to prevent all the manipulative people from affecting their lives. In other words, if you are able to set healthy boundaries, the people who are around, you won't have a chance to manipulate you. The art is linked to the fact that you won't open up and allow manipulative people have credit over your efforts.

## TRY TO FIT IN

As you cope up or live with manipulative people, you need to keep re-inventing yourself and try as much as possible to fit in. One of the significant characteristics of manipulative people is that they like a situation where you are using all your efforts to please them. For instance, they will love a job where you come and clean their houses and make them happy. They will want a position where you wake up in the morning and prepare their offices for them. They will also prefer a situation where you leave your duties and ensure that they are first fixed. You don't have to meet all their, please. However, you can try and fit in their desires but don't allow them to carry you. The aspect is linked to the fact that their ideas are aimed at manipulating you. Also, if you avoid doing what they want, your life might be miserable. The aspect is linked to the fact that most of these manipulative people are your bosses. In other words, they are the kind of people you need to work under so as you can excel. Thus, try and fit in their rules but don't give in to their demands. In other words, you can look for different ways of fixing their applications rather than using the techniques as well as the strategies they have identified. The aspect is critical in the sense that your actions will act as eye-openers in the desire to change. If you can achieve their demands using other means they may end fearing you. The aspect is linked to the fact that they will understand that they aren't the only people who can come up with such ideas. Thus, they will be cautious in terms of their actions and demands. However, you don't have to show them how sharp you are. They may end up ill-treating you. However, if you are wise in the way you conduct things, they may fear you and avoid cases where they will ill-treat you. The aspect is linked to the fact that there will be a sense of self-respect that will emerge in between you.

## Chapter 8

# HYPNOSIS AND SELF-HYPNOSIS

Hypnosis refers to an induction of a state of consciousness where a person loses their power of voluntary actions and is highly responsive to any direction as well as suggestion. It is one of the useful therapy that allows one to suppress their memories and will enable the modification of their behaviors. Self-hypnosis, on the other hand, refers to an instinctively happening state of mind that can be illustrated as an elevated state of fixated concentration. In other words, it changes the way a person thinks, kick out bad habits as well as control themselves. It is one of the means of introducing the art of relaxations and distressing the day to day life. The two aspects are critical in the sense that they allow one mind to re-write or rather reprogram the subconscious. The element is crucial in the sense that it will enable one to relax and bypass the issues that are affecting someone hence introducing some positive mindsets.

In most cases, the ideas as well as aspects instilled in one`s minds are positive and encourages one to re-think more and act differently. It is one of the best ways of enhancing the efficacy of self-suggestion and plays the due role of being the suggester and the suggested. In other words, the aspect allows one mind to indicate to itself the things that ought to be carried out or be done for a solution to be viable. Thus, the two aspects are very crucial in life.

Take a look at some of the importance of both Hypnosis and Self-hypnosis.

## IMPROVING DEEP SLEEP

Several studies have been used to explore the effect of hypnosis on one`s sleep. In most of these studies, the participants were asked to report back on how well or poorly they slept after hypnosis. In most cases, victims who have sleep issues have reported improving after anesthesia. One of the effects of hypnosis is that it allows the minds of an individual to relax and empties all the negative thinking. The aspect is critical in the sense that it will enable one to develop some understanding of cooling as well as relaxation. Thus one is able to sleep well and wakes up while more active. It is worth noting that sleeping is a state of mind. Also, the art of sleeping is directly proportional to the level of one's tiredness. In other words, if one is tired, there are chances that they will be able to sleep well. However, with age, the aspect of sleeping tends to reduce. The inactivity that tends to increase with age tends to decrease the art of sleeping. In other words, the elders in society have sleep issues. The technique can be linked to the fact that most of them are inactive during the day, and they may remain active for the entire day. Thus, their rate of sleeping may tend to lower. However, with hypnosis, such cases are rare. The art is linked to the fact that hypnosis allows the mind of an individual to be emptied and re-written in a new way. The technique creates some sense of relaxation that will enable one to sleep well. One of the merits of hypnosis is that it doesn't have any side effects. It is worth noting that numerous drugs are used to induce sleep in an individual.

In most cases, some of these drugs are addictive, such that people who are used to them can't get sleep without taking such drugs. The other aspect is that apart from addiction, the drugs may increase the hangover issues that affect people who are addicted to drug abuse. Thus it one of the safest means of solving problems of sleep.

## IT EASES SYMPTOMS OF IRRITABLE BOWEL SYNDROME.

Various studies have been carried out to identify the effects of hypnosis in one's life. There have been reports that clients with Irritable bowel syndrome have greatly improved after a consecutive 12 weeks of hypnosis. It is worth noting that the improvement occurred even after months of inductive therapy. Hypnosis, as well as self-hypnosis, are critical in the sense that they reduce the cost of healthcare to the entire society. The other merit is that it is one of the therapies that doesn't attract any attention in terms of causing chaos. However, hypnosis creates an environment that creates an excellent mental picture that tends to capture the attention of one's mind hence bringing a healing effect. The art of emptying one's mind and allowing the state of relaxation will enable one to attract more positivity. The art of being positive creates some sense of enjoyment in one's mind hence bringing about a healing effect.

## CALMING NERVES

The nerves of an individual are always active. However, there are situations where the minds of an individual need to relax and lower anxiety. In most cases, when one is afraid, their hair stands, some may sweat or even shaking. At such moments, the nerves are active, and there are cases where operations are required for such nerves to be examined. However, hypnosis helps the mind as well as the nerves to relax and brings down the art of being anxious. The other aspect that affects the brain of an individual is expectations.

In most cases, the expectations that people have tend to cause some sense of alarm in an individual. The aspect may be so intense that the individual may develop what is called anxiety-related disorder. The victim is always anxious about what will happen in the future. The art causes the minds to over-think and in the long –run increases the trait if being over-expectant. However, hypnosis is one of the therapies that are effective in lowering anxiety.

## TREATMENT OF LIFE-STYLE DISEASES SUCH AS HYPERTENSION

Most of the life-style diseases that affect people tend to originate from the state of mind. For instance, anxiety increases the rate at which the heart pumps blood. In most cases, when the price of pumping blood increases, the pressure of blood increases within the narrow vessels. The aspect can be dangerous as if the pressure reaches the capillaries in the head. Blood pressure is thus a state of mind that needs to be challenged. In other words, the incidence of mental illness is directly proportional to the increase in blood pressure. Therefore, the treatment of blood of these conditions requires more attention to the minds. The aspect means that if the accounts of such an individual are allowed to relax, the chances are that cases of blood pressure lower, and there is a healing effect that is noted.

## MEMORY IMPROVEMENT

As outlined earlier, one of the aspects of hypnosis is

that it allows the minds of an individual to refresh or rather to be re-programmed. The re-creation is essential in improving one's memory. It is worth noting that once the accounts are upgraded, there is a healing effect that is instilled. In most cases, the negative aspect of the brain tends to lower. It is worth noting that a positive mind brings some sense of relaxation in the accounts. One thinks well hence the ability to remember many aspects. For instance, in a class, the difference between a bright student and a dull one is the attitude over a particular subject. For example, students who fear mathematics tend to develop some sense of negativity towards teaching.

In most cases, the victim can't pass on such a subject. The aspect is linked to the fact that the victim has developed a negative mindset that robs one's ability to remember. On the other hand, positive students tend to have an increased ability to recognize aspects of the same subject. The element causes one to have a better memory. Thus, the art of developing a positive mind0setn after a session of hypnosis plays a critical role in boosting the mind of an individual.

## IMPROVES CONCENTRATION AND FOCUS

A relaxed mind is more attentive than a tired one. One of the most important aspects of hypnosis is that it allows the mind to relax and reprogram itself. In most cases, as the brain reprogram itself, some points are eliminated. Most of the elements that are removed are more contradictory ideas as well as issues that hinder a person's prosperity. After a session of relaxation, or rather hypnosis, the minds are rejuvenated and less depressed. The feeling of anxiety lowers, and one gets ready for grasping more ideas. In other words, the art of concentration and focus improves after a session of hypnosis. The art of phobia and other mental related disorders are eliminated. Also, the art of healing gastrointestinal disorders as well as high blood pressure causes the minds to relax and focus on other vital issues. It is one of the best therapy of topics such as low self-esteem as well as stress disorders. Thus, the minds are allowed to relax and heal. The rejuvenations give the mind time to heal and prepare for learning. Therefore, if you are willing to improve on your studies, you need to have some sessions of hypnosis and improve on your focus, let alone concentration.

*Chapter 9*

# EMOTIONAL MANIPULATION (HOW ITS MECHANISM WORKS)

Some people are always lucky in that they can get what they want at any time the need arises. Sometimes they do so at the expense of others, this, however, is achieved via access to the emotional bank. They can influence your thoughts or emotions to their advantage and leave you a victim and vulnerable. Emotional manipulation, therefore, involves access to someone and influencing them for information or any other favors through their emotions. It sucks and it is unethical once you realize what has been done to you. Do not get confused, there are two sides to emotional manipulation. There is an ethical and unethical side. What feels like betrayal is the unethical one. However, mastering emotional intelligence plays a barrier role to these manipulations and keeps you in a safe spot. In this chapter, the focus is on how emotional manipulation is attained and the mechanisms behind it.

## OWNING SPACE

The main aim of emotional manipulation is to make you lose control of your emotions. It will involve making you stagger with emotions which on the other hand will make you even more vulnerable. Advantage will be taken and they will access you and get all they wanted from you. If there existed a lock to the emotions, I am sure everybody would have their emotions locked away and unlocked only to intimate relationships or where your emotions will be valued. To make sure you are off the steering with your emotions, manipulators will invite you to a place where they know it is new to you but familiar to them. This will keep you off balance, the new environment will give him or her the dominance and feeling of being in control. You are new to the place and the manipulator will take advantage of the window between adaptability and regaining control.

## YOUR WORDS AGAINST YOU

How you talk or react speaks volumes and emotions can be passed along. Manipulators like a talkative person since it is easier to access them due to the link provided; speaking out. If you are the introvert type or a conservative person it takes more effort to make you open up. Introverts would require tailored questions that will be well planned and will give you away from one by one. The manipulator makes sure the questions are aimed at the emotional state. Personal questions will open you up and you will start speaking with feelings, this is an indicator that manipulation is taking place and it is working. By asking simple and tailored questions that mostly are personal or involve something we like hobbies, interests among others will lead to saturation with emotions. A master manipulator will take advantage of the situation and make us of the questions to establish your beliefs, strengths, and weaknesses without you realizing it.

## GUILT

Kind-hearted victims are easily vulnerable to emotional manipulation. Guilt will be used against you, especially if you are so sensitive you may end up giving in to their demands. Guilt will either make you give in or feel bad about yourself. For instance, you may both agree on something and when the time comes to complete the deal the manipulators will pretend to forget or even act as victims of your actions. By doing so they will be finding your soft spot and once they find it will be the target of manipulation. Guilt and sympathy will be served to you, if you are not strong enough you will fall for the play. They will influence you through that guilt since you will be under their spell and since you now believe they are the victims you will do all they ask just to make sure your 'victims' do not suffer anymore.

## POSITIVE AND NEGATIVE EMOTIONS

Emotions of sadness or happiness can also be a pathway for emotional manipulation. An emotional manipulator will play with your psychology, he or she will show you that what you might be going through is nothing compared to what they have going on in their lives. By doing this, they try to exalt you and win your trust. If you fall for that and believe there are more needy people than you in the world then you will loosen up and think that you are selfish. You will no longer focus on your big problem, rather you will focus on their 'big unfortunate events' since you will now feel pitiful. Once you trust them, then you give them a key to your emotional bank and surely they will use it against you. Once you trust them, you might end up offering yourself to assist them, that, however, was their plan from the start; they will have attained their goal.

## ANGER

Anger is another emotion that can be used to induce emotional manipulation. Some people are natural peacemakers, they avoid confrontations and conflicts in all ways possible. Once a manipulator realizes you are this type of person, he or she will use anger, aggressive language or raise his or her voice or even drop several threats. These aggressive techniques are tailored just to make tick. The secret behind this aggressive approach is to induce fear and discomfort so that you can give in hastily without taking a second to think through. Once you give in to their demands they now get control over you and now can manipulate you in whatever direction or way that pleases them. They use this opportunity to get what they wanted from you since you will be cooperative earing to bring another instance of acute aggression.

## SELF-DISCIPLINE AND CONFIDENCE

Being self-driven and confident is a very strong barrier to the effects of emotional manipulation. With the right mindset, you become less vulnerable to emotional manipulation attacks. Insecure and sensitive people are the easiest target for emotional manipulators. They are easily spotted and accessible, they put their needs behind those of others and are often feeling the need to please. All a manipulator needs is to be caring, sensitive and with an urge to help out. The needy part of sensitive people exposes them and the emotional manipulator will see it as a gate pass to influencing your thoughts, perceptions, and feelings to his or her advantage. With time the emotions break open and they are exploited easily since the manipulator was disguised as a caring and sensitive person. As the saying goes, birds of a feather flock together; the feeling of sharing the same trait will open them up for manipulation without their knowledge.

## SURPRISES

Negative surprises is also another mechanism used to keep people off balance. When bombarded with the new unexpected news that comes with a limited timeframe will lead to panic. As you panic, you get little time or none to think of a counter move. They may be good enough to trap you with suggestions as they pretend to help yet it is a plan made to make you unstable both psychologically and emotionally. Once you become unstable and overwhelmed by the sudden change of events it becomes their opportunity to influence your decisions and any other emotion they are interested in. They may even consider making more moves that will bind your relationship with him, her or them so that they can utilize that window of opportunity created by the panic moment. You may not realize it since they appear to be assisting whereas they are using you for their benefits.

## CRITICISM

Criticism is also a tool for emotional manipulation. The manipulator will say bad things of you, ridicule you or even dismiss you. He or she will make sure her mission of dismantling you succeeds. Once you have had enough you end up off balance and believe they are much superior compared to the inferior you. You will feel so down and their opinions will stick. Once you are in this state you are vulnerable. The manipulator will make sure you understand that you can never be good at anything no matter what you do or invest in. This will get into you and you will be emotionally distressed. You will feel hurt and not worthy of anyone's help. They will then pretend to have answers to your problems. He or she will give you tips and suggestions that are so genuine looking and constructive. Once these well-outlined answers transform you and get you out of it they threw you will worship them. Once they have your attention they can then make you do what they want or influence you.

## DOUBT

Doubt and uncertainty are also other forms of leverage in emotional manipulation. You will receive a silent treatment until you start doubting your actions or words that you may have used the last time. The manipulators will do this deliberately to stir up the feeling of doubt, once you give in and break the silence by acting as the cause of the silence treatment will be a good chance to be taken advantage of. This creates a window of opportunity and they will manipulate you.

## IGNORANCE

Pretending to be ignorant of your duties will also get things done. You may want to do something but you want it done by someone else, let us say your spouse. She or he will note something is off and will try to make it right but you pretend to be good with it but since they know it has to be right they will do it anyway.

## Chapter 10

# HOW TO LEARN TO USE MANIPULATION TO YOUR ADVANTAGE

Manipulation is something that we cannot master overnight. The closer you get to a person the easier the process of manipulation becomes. Making people fall into your traps and flow with your ideas making it seem it was theirs in the first place is a manipulative move. Getting things done efficiently would be our greatest achievement but when we get assistance and it is done perfectly, we feel more graceful and happy. With the power of manipulation which would take some time to master, you can swing things around to fit your needs and desires. In this chapter, the focus is on the ways that can be apprehended and used to make sure you gain the skills of manipulation and use them accordingly; to suit your needs. Manipulation strategies will require some cold-heartedness since may involve hurting other peoples' emotions without caring. The focus is on what you can get and the method does not necessarily care about what your emotions are or what might be at stake.

## EMOTIONAL INTELLIGENCE

Learn emotional intelligence and practice it. To access people's actions and feelings, emotions make it easier. Emotions are able to access the mind; subconsciously and we react subconsciously. Unless you have mastered the art of emotional intelligence and self-discipline you cannot avoid an attack on the emotions' bank; the subconscious mind. The subconscious mind will act fast and without the awareness and consent of the conscious mind. This, however, makes the bridge to manipulation; the manipulator will now be in a position to access your feelings and play around with them so that you can tune to the song being played. Make sure you harness the power of emotional intelligence and be in a position to radiate the products of the same. Once you master that, manipulation will become a piece of cake and you will influence people's thoughts, feelings, and emotions to your liking.

## CHARMS AND FLIRTS

Master the art of charms and flirts. People that like you without effort are likely to do anything to get noticed by you; the charming guy. Use charms to gain popularity and love from people, let people talk about how good you are and likable. To this, trait and image made out there add a touch of fluttery to spice things up; you will prepare lands that you can garden any time as long as you use the right approach to smoothen things. Manipulating people that have a crush on you becomes easy and when you keep your sexuality off the table and flirt, you will access control of people who are vulnerable. People with self-esteem are mostly people-pleasing and therefore when you show interest they will easily fall into your arms. Use this opportunity to make them work towards your goal or assist you in any way that pleases you.

## INVEST IN SELF-CONFIDENCE

Learn the power of being confident in yourself. People are likely to believe you more when you are confident in yourself and what you say. To win people overuse the right posture and words accompanied by a handful of confidence and magic will happen. What you say to them will not matter, your actions rather will be the target to scrutiny and once you win them over you will have their loyalty to yourself. Once they believe that what you do is for their benefit and you let it stick to them with a lot of confidence, they will participate even though it is against their desires.

## ACT

Be an actor, pretend to be something you are not so as to fit in. Learn how to use trust to open up people. Act needy and tell someone a very private and personal experience, they will be triggered to share theirs. It takes a lot of courage and trust to let go off of some of such private issues. Once you win the trust of the individual you are a step ahead in manipulation. The victim might not know the validity of the story if you act right and blend in feelings with the story and experience. The victim also might not be aware of the manipulation since the exchange of the experiences.

## EMPATHY

Empathy will make people trust you since you seem to understand what they feel. Understanding people and giving them a shoulder to cry on is emotional support. People will trust you with their problems and insecurities as long as you maintain the relationship. Be a good listener and show care and understanding. The feeling of having someone by your side in times of crisis will make you do all to maintain him or her. Use the opportunity to make sure they tune to your beat. They might not realize they are helping out rather them it will be an act of kindness.

## APPRENTICESHIP

Working closely with a master manipulator will also get you a ton of skills in manipulation. You will learn by observing and apprenticeship. Theoretical knowledge learned sometimes proves hard to apply to the field. Therefore, learning the way to manipulate people under an expert as you watch it being done, chances are that you will become very good at it. You learn even more modified techniques that will not be covered in the theoretical class. Practice makes perfect therefore learning under an expert and practicing what he or she does will get you started. If you are this lucky to have a manipulator around make use of him or her to achieve the skills of manipulation.

## MIRRORING

Mirroring actions or postures of the target individuals may bring synchronization between you two. Manipulators try to imitate your actions and posture both voluntary and involuntary ones. This will help open up the target individual and also show them that you are aware of their insecurities if any exists. Not only does mirroring involve the postures but also the words said. Repeating what has been said lastly with an agreeing tone will show that you were attentive and interested in the topic. Showing interest in what they have to say will make sure they do the same when your turn comes.

*Chapter 11*

# WHAT COMMUNICATION AND VERBAL SKILLS NEED TO BE DEVELOPED TO IMPROVE PERSUASION AND MANIPULATION SKILLS?

There is nothing as important as being able to communicate effectively. One has to be able to verbally communicate in a way that people around them understand. People will believe and put their trust in someone who has effective communication skills. This is because they know how to speak to everyone depending on their levels of understanding. There are those types of competencies that one must have in order for them to be able to communicate effectively. A manipulator needs to have verbal skills in order for them to be able to communicate effectively with their victims

Being able to speak is more than just speaking. You are required to ensure that you convey the information you need to communicate to someone and they understand it. When they understand and respond the way you would want them to, that is when you will be able to say that you have communicated. It is important for a manipulator to understand that in order for them to use the communication skills to manipulate their victims without experiencing any communication problem.

Fortunately, all these skills can be learned or nurtured. Manipulators need to, therefore, ensure that they have the required skills for them to use when manipulating people. I have discussed some of the skills below.

## LISTENING SKILLS

A manipulator needs to be a good listener if they want to be able to communicate with other people. They need to pay very close attention to the people they want to manipulate in order for them to be able to learn about their weaknesses and be able to use them against them. Active listening is very important since you will be able to capture all the required information for your own benefit. It is important for a manipulator to be able to learn the language that the victims understand. This will be of great help in ensuring that they do not use a complex language, which they will not understand.

An active listener will be able to listen to the recipient without judging them. When the manipulator judges the recipient, they will not be able to trust them. This will make them keep the information you need for themselves. To win their trust, you need to make sure that you pay attention to them as they speak. By doing all this, they will be able to give the information you require not knowing that you will use the same information to manipulate them.

## OPEN COMMUNICATION

Open communication is all about first impressions. The way one communicates with you the first time you meet helps you to judge their ability to communicate or not. How a manipulator communicates the first time they meet people will, therefore, determine whether they will be able to manipulate the recipient or not. A manipulator, therefore, needs to ensure that they have the required ability to communicate with the recipients. This will be of great help when they want to win them over to their side. Being open with communication will help you to be able to ensure that the victims gain their trust in you which will make them also open up to you. Your goal as a manipulator is to ensure that they give you as much information as they can which you will later use against them. This will make it easy for you to be able to persuade them or manipulate them.

## REINFORCEMENT

The use of reinforcement is a very common technique when one wants to use communication effectively. Manipulators can use it to improve their communication with the victim. They will be required to use encouraging words as well as gestures that are non-verbal when communicating with the victims in order for you to be able to make friends with them. This helps you as a manipulator to build a great rapport with them, which enables you to win their trust.

You will engage them in discussions and encourage them to keep opening up to you. Whenever they are down, you will need to be there to reassure them that all will be well. This will help you a lot when manipulating them since they will feel obligated to help you since you were also there for them when they needed you. You will, therefore, be able to easily manipulate them without experiencing any challenges.

## QUESTIONING

It is through questions that we are able to get information about various things. You will be able to get clarity for various issues when you question. A manipulator needs this skill too. They will use it to question their victims and get all the information they may need from them. This will give you a chance to be able to know their strengths and weaknesses which will in return help you to manipulate them. As a manipulator, you can choose to use either open or closed questions. A closed question is those that will give you either a yes or a no. an open one is one that the victim will need to explain their answers or discuss them. The best type of question to use in this case is the open one. This is because it will give you room to give you as much information as possible. A manipulator should, therefore, utilize these questions to ensure that they use the best opportunity to manipulate their victims.

## REFLECTING AND CLARITY

Reflection is normally used when one needs clarity on the things another person said. They translate the information given by another person into a simpler language that they can understand. A manipulator can use this opportunity to distort the information they give to the manipulator. They will ensure that the victim understands what manipulators can use to manipulate them. The information they give their victims is contrary to what the speaker said. This will help them to be able to easily manipulate the victim into following what they want.

## NEGOTIATION SKILLS

Negotiation skills refer to helping people to reconcile with or agree with each other's ideas. Negotiation is meant to make sure that people are living in peace and harmony especially at the workplace. A manipulator can use negotiation skills to make their victims agree with him. He will share ideas and ensure that the people they want to manipulate agree to them. This will work very well since most of the ideas they will be sharing will be manipulative. They will be for their own selfish gain. By the time, the victims realize it; they will have already been manipulated and will not be able to come out of it easily.

## IMPORTANCE OF DEVELOPING COMMUNICATION AND VERBAL SKILLS IN MANIPULATION

Communication and verbal skills are important for any manipulator. This is because of how one communicates dictates whether they will be able to manipulate their victims or not.

Through communication, a manipulator will be able to derive information from their victims which they to manipulate them later.

Through communication, a manipulator is able to learn the strengths and weaknesses of their victims, which they use to manipulate them. They will use their weaknesses to make them follow all the instructions that they give. Manipulators do not people who are aware of themselves because it is not easy to manipulate them.

The manipulators also use communication to earn the trust of their victims. They have to use a good language, which they understand in order for their victims to trust them. These manipulators will be there to comfort their victims when they need them with encouraging words. By doing this, they are able to win their trust and manipulate them the sympathy in the future. The manipulators need to, therefore, use the best language for them to win people to their side.

Another importance of communication is that manipulators are good negotiators. They will use the appropriate language to make their victims fall prey to their trick to manipulate them. They will make sure that every information they get from the victim against them.

A manipulator will also be able to give clear instruction, which will be understood by their victims. For a manipulator to be able to manipulate them, they have to ensure that they understand the instructions and follow them as expected.

They will also be able to use communication and verbal skills to influence the victims of manipulation to their side. The ability to influence them is what will help them to win their trust, which in return enables them to be able to manipulate them.

A manipulator should, therefore, ensure that they learn the communication and verbal skills in order for them to be able to manipulate their victims effectively. This is because their art of manipulation is the one that will determine whether they will be able to manipulate them or not. Without communication, a manipulator would not be able to persuade, negotiate and even question the victims into manipulating them. It is therefore important for manipulators to sharpen their verbal communication in order for them to be able to succeed in manipulation.

## Chapter 12

# HOW TO USE MANIPULATION TO MANIPULATE, PERSUADE AND INFLUENCE PEOPLE

We all find manipulating other people's minds unethical. This is because we consider it as playing with people's feelings as well as thoughts and emotions in order for it to benefit us alone. That is considered a very selfish move. Manipulators know how to play their cards well. They will make sure that they use all the available techniques to manipulate the targeted people. Whether manipulation is unethical or not mostly depends on an individual. This is because we are the ones with the final decision as to whether we should allow them to manipulate us or not.

One is therefore required to evaluate themselves every often in order for them to ensure that they have the required skills for them to be able to avoid manipulators. In this chapter, I am going to discuss some of the many manipulation techniques that one can use to manipulate, persuade and influence people.

## FEAR AND RELIEF TECHNIQUE

Fear and relief is a technique that is said to be very efficient when it comes to playing with other people's emotions. A manipulator is only required to instill some fear on an individual, which immediately makes them vulnerable. At the time when they are vulnerable, the manipulator does anything they want in their favor. The manipulator manipulates the individual at this point since they know that the victim will do anything to get out of the fearful situation.

The only challenge that the manipulator might encounter when using this technique is identifying the things that make them fear. They will, therefore, need to keep fearful situations to the every now and then until when they will identify it. The manipulators succeed in this situation since most people hate situations that make them fear. They would anything to make sure that they get out of the situation.

An example of how this technique is used is when the media wants to keep its viewers following the channel. They will put up a juicy headline, which will keep the viewers glued on the screen waiting for it. The reporter will then keep reporting that they need to keep watching the program in order for them to get the juicy news. Everyone will keep watching in the hope that the program will still come.

With fear and relief techniques, the manipulator is expected to instill fear until when they see that the manipulator is about to give up. It is at this point that they will be able to relieve them of the pressure that they are going through which makes them less stressful. The fearful situation that they have been through makes them obey the manipulator's orders anytime they give them since they would not want to go back to the situation they were in before.

## GUILTY APPROACH TECHNIQUE

Through the guilty approach technique, the manipulator makes their prey guilty in order for them to be able to manipulate them. They will make sure that they blame them for things they did not do. One will want to compensate the manipulator without the knowledge that they will are about to be manipulated. A manipulator has to however make sure that their target is someone who is prone to feeling guilty.

Once you make the person guilty, you will be able to swing them in any direction since they are willing to do anything to make sure that you forget the things that they did to you. It works so perfectly since according to the victim, they will compensate for the moments that they were not nice to you but for the manipulator, it will be time to use them for their selfish gain. The guilt approach technique, therefore, works so well when one wants to influence other people since the victim will be feeling an obligation to make it up to you for the trouble they caused you. Little do they know that the manipulator was waiting for such a moment to strike?

## PLAYING THE VICTIM

This type of technique is somehow similar to the guilty approach technique. Playing the victim may however work against you if not careful when implementing it. You would be required to ensure that you do not overuse it. The trick is normally to ensure that you make the targeted person feel bad about a given situation. You will be required to ensure that the person actually made the mistake but for you, playing the victim shall be an exaggeration. The victim will feel bad about it and will want to compensate it by doing something different for you. They will, therefore, be nice to you, which will help the manipulator to use them to achieve her goals.

## LOVE BOMBING TECHNIQUE

We all like it when we feel loved by the people around us. We will all appreciate it when the people around us make us feel appreciated and loved. That is why manipulators use love and attention to manipulate people.

This technique is mostly used for the purposes of manipulating people emotionally. A manipulator will mostly give a lot of attention to their targeted individual. They will show them a lot of affection, which would make them, not suspect anything from the manipulator. By doing this, they will be setting up a trap for them. They will be laying the ground, which they will use for their manipulation purposes. When the right time comes, they are able to easily execute their plan. This means that by the time they realize that you are manipulating them; they will have already been influenced to a place of no return.

## BRIBERY TECHNIQUE

This technique is said to work like a charm. This is because you will reward someone out of nowhere and they will automatically want to return the favor in a different way. It is an easy job since you are only required to find out what your victim needs and you get them exactly that. You will only be expected to look as genuine as possible. This will make the person really happy such that if you ever mention that you need anything, they will not hesitate to get it for you. By doing this, you will be able to make demands from them as many times as possible without them noticing that you are manipulating them. Through this technique, you will have influenced people to your system, which they may find it difficult to exit.

## BECOMING A GOOD LISTENER

A manipulator knows that people need good listeners in their lives. A good listener earns people's trust so easily. This is because they will come out as being very caring and concerned. This makes the victim trust them completely. A manipulator cannot manipulate people before gaining their trust. Once you have their trust, it will be very easy to manipulate them. You will only be required to discuss with them a few things that you may be going through and without even questioning, they will reciprocate for it since you were there for them before. Through the trust, the manipulator will be able to manipulate them for a long time without the victim noticing.

In as much as a manipulator uses these skills to manipulate, persuade and influence people, they all need to be good in some skills. Some of the skills have been discussed below.

- They need to have excellent verbal communication skills. No one will listen to someone who cannot communicate clearly. You would need to be able to express yourself well if at all you want people to listen to you. Most manipulators have mastered this skill very well which helps them to prey on people without them noticing. When one is good in communication, they are able to easily prey on the victims with the language that they understand. The victims will, therefore, understand the manipulator very well and follow all the instructions given without knowing that they are in the trap of being manipulated.

- For a manipulator to be able to manipulate and persuade people, they should look good before them. Your way of dressing and the way you present yourself tells a lot about you. People will only take you seriously when you look good. You will be able to earn their trust easily. People are normally impressed by people who dress nicely, who are well kept and also who have manners. They will easily like them and listen to them and in the process trust them. Once trust kicks in, the manipulators are able to easily persuade them as well as influence them in the direction that they want.

- When you are conversant about psychology, you will be able to read people's minds. You will be able to know how they feel, how they will react to certain things and also their mood. Knowing all this will be of great help in ensuring that you use their weaknesses to your advantage. You will be able to manipulate them without their knowledge.

## Chapter 13

# THE BEST TECHNIQUES OF PERSUASION

From the previous chapter, we have already gathered what manipulation is and how best you may use manipulation to your advantage. The chapter was keen enough to take us through the facets of manipulation. This chapter, however, focuses its radar on the art of persuasion. Before we indulge further into the major facets of persuasion, we will first have to comprehend the meaning of persuasion. Persuasion refers to the psychological influence which affects the choice that an individual ought to make. With persuasion, an individual is often inclined to make you buy his or her school of thought in a bid to change your thought process. In order for one to effectively achieve persuasion, there are a number of things that need to be put in mind. When we are able to go beyond the natural human framework and get a grasp of what moves others, then you are in a position to achieve effective persuasion. This is because you are aware of the pressure points and how best to manipulate them.

When exploiting the art of persuasion, there are various pointers that can come in handy. These are:

## MIMICKING

As human beings of reason, we tend to vary from one individual to another. The diversity of this is what makes us appear in the discrepancy of others. Owing to this particular fact, you will find that as individuals, we are more drawn to be warm and welcoming to those people who exhibit the same characteristics as us. It could be a physical trait or just the way an individual carries themselves out. This type of technique is said to elicit positive feelings that go a mile when it comes to persuasion. When an individual has the feelings of liking towards someone, he or she is in a position to be swayed by your influence.

In a bid to elaborate on this particular type of technique, we are going to employ the use of this scenario. In the hotel industry, especially in the most advanced and high-end ones, you will find that the allocation of a waiter is dependent on the customer. High-end hotels in the industry have high customer feedback and thus they tend to treat their clients in a manner that suggests so. A client, for instance, would be allocated a particular type of waiter who matches their description. For instance, French waiters are renowned for their exquisite service. Putting the client first is at the top of the list when it comes to this particular field. Many professionals have succeeded in this area owing to the manner in which they treated clients. This is because of the clients re the main source of business. Putting the client into consideration goes a notch higher to even saying the exact words that the client has said. With this, they are able to gather that you have aptly decoded what they meant.

In order to accurately achieve this particular technique, an individual ought to do a number of things. First, he or she may consider doing in-depth research into the particular field of the question in order to see to it that what is required of them is met. Before you are able to achieve persuasion by the use of this technique, one ought to be well versed with the individual that he or she ought to persuade. This type of expertise should be keen enough to make sure that it elicits major points that may come in handy during the process of persuasion.

## SOCIAL PROOF

When it comes to persuasion, social proof has repeatedly proven its dominance. Before we go deeper into the technique, we first need to gather the meaning of social proof. Social proof refers to the process by which an individual's feelings and thought process are affected by the way other people have reacted to the same issue. When it comes to social influence. An individual who is the persuader, draw his or her basis from the acts that others have engaged in time and again. It could be the norm. With human beings, the danger that occurs is the feeling cf wanting to be associated with a group of people. Human beings want to accrue a sense of belonging either to a group of people or to a particular act and this is what puts them at a higher risk of being influenced easily.

Employing social proof when persuading an individual will mean that you have a basis of a norm that has been used repeatedly by the people whom we consider to be in the same class. This basis must be something that most people engage in and not a few numbers. Take, for instance, there are newbies in the estate who are looking for service providers. This newbie would first be inclined to know what other people in the estate are using. Although they might not settle on the same option as the rest of the estate, this will be somewhat a buildup on to what choice they may choose to settle upon. Rather they may end up embracing what others have used. With this technique, the trick lies whereby you ought to create a distinction in the manner in which an individual sees himself or herself as per against others. You will only achieve persuasion by convincing this individual that the desired option is one that has been embraced by a large group of individuals.

## RECIPROCITY

When it comes to this type of technique, one needs to understand that a good deed was done to another individual no matter how remote, tends to go a long way. From the wording of it, reciprocity refers to the process by which an individual is able to respond to a good deed by performing a good deed in return. With this type of technique, we will find that most people fail to notice at its onset not until you are obligated to return the favor. In the world today, it is almost as rare as the sun rising from the west as it is to find someone who will extend feelings of warmness and care towards you. Save the people whom we are closely related, we tend to feel differently when an individual who is not even in your circle of friendship extends warm-hearted feelings.

The feeling of obligation arises as a result of being extended a good deed by an individual. This is the result of being extended with feelings of warmness. At this point, you are in a position to persuade the individual in the manner that you wish. This is because he or she would be obliged to follow in the direction of the wind. It should be noted that this particular type of technique ought to be time cautious. This is because the implication of reciprocity does not last forever. There are limits to this timeline and one should be cautious enough to make sure that these limits are not exploited. With the passing of more time, it weakens the wave of reciprocity.

In order to achieve this particular type of technique, an individual ought to play in the tone of offers and obligations. If your offer is worth it, then it raises an obligation effect on the other hand. Thus creating a win situation.

## CONSISTENCY AND COMMITMENT

This type of technique is wired on an already formed perception. An individual is in a position to settle on a particular choice. The choice that this individual picks would be pegged on him or her for as far as they go. From the wording of it, consistency and commitment refer to the fact that an individual is in a position to make a choice and stick to it with sheer determination and perseverance. When it comes to persuasion, not all techniques may work and you may find that you hit rock bottom once or twice in your venture. When this happens, it is not advisable to give up. Consistency is what builds our character in almost every facet in life. This type of technique is vast in a manner that cuts across various fields not limited to the field of education and business. The first approach to an individual for purposes of convincing them may or may not end up in a manner that you wish. The first approach is often one that is characterized by rejection and in some cases mental torture. The best way to respond to this type of instance is by not giving up. The second encounter of individuals who first rejected your idea will see to it that you have an audience who understands what you are talking about.

The talk of consistency and commitment is one that does not go down the throat easily. This is because these are the most subtle facets to embrace because they tend to take a toll on an individual. You can imagine getting rejected severally. In order to achieve commitment, an individual ought to operate in a manner that is relentless.

## Chapter 14

# PRACTICAL EXAMPLES OF HOW TO MANIPULATE ANYONE

From the previous chapter, we have gathered what persuasion is and the various techniques that may be employed in a bid to persuade somebody. Chapter 11 was keen to elicit the process of using manipulation in order to achieve what you want. This chapter is keen to relate to chapter 11 in that it brings out the practicality of the whole process of manipulation. At this juncture, we have already gathered what manipulation is. We have seen that manipulation entails the skillful application of various pointers that work in a bid to achieve inclination towards a preferred specific school of thought. When we practice manipulation, it is often because we desire something which is not in the scope of our reach. Owing to this, we have to make others do the work for us involuntary and unconsciously. Most of the time when individuals are not aware of the manipulation that overwhelms them until in the later stages in life.

There exist various reasons that an individual may want to manipulate someone in order to achieve. Regardless of the reasons, an individual ought to operate in a manner that suggests that he or she is in charge of the whole process. In order to be able to achieve manipulation, there are a number of things that an individual ought to put in mind. Because this is a practical expedition, we are going to go as remote as possible.

## MASTERING ACTING SKILLS

With manipulation, the biggest part of your venture is premised upon the idea of misrepresenting the actual facts. In order to achieve this, an individual must be in the brackets of the know-how of acting. Acting majorly implies that you are behaving in a manner that is not in the presiding set of events but you are still keen enough to make sure that the other party is not aware of this. With acting, there come various emotions that ought to be put into consideration. In order to fully master these emotions, you have to make sure that you are keen enough to elicit these emotions when need be.

The exhibiting of emotions is a crucial facet in this juncture that can be mastered through the taking up of acting classes. When you are on the verge of attending these particular classes, you ought to maintain the utmost secrecy as to your intentions of the class. Emotions are a big part of the manipulation and how best you play with them will determine how best you achieve manipulation.

Another way in which an individual can be able to mater his or her skills of acting is through indulging in public speaking and debate. With the debate, you are able to focus your thoughts in a more direct manner in that what you are saying will be synchronized with the emotions that you are exhibiting. Public speaking creates the culture of organizing one's ideas in a manner that is advantageous when it comes to explaining these thoughts. When engaging in debating activities, you are in a position to master how best you can either convince the opponents to buy from your school of thought since you believe it is the best. When you are able to achieve to make others find your wants as convincing, then you are in a position to achieve manipulation.

## ESTABLISHING SIMILARITIES

This can be linked to mimicking. When you are encountering an individual for the novel time, you are in a position whereby you are seeing their characteristics for the first time. These characteristics ought to work to your advantage. For instance, you may encounter an individual and the major pointers that you need to look at are in the physicality of the individual. This includes the way an individual talks, the way he or she walks or carries themselves out. When you are in a position to have a grasp of this, then you can now start working on the. Persuasiveness will commence with how you take advantage of these factors. For instance, the way an individual speaks is his or her intonation. Responding in a manner that suggests a similarity between then intonations goes a mile when it comes to manipulation. An individual is more inclined to listen to you if you are calm and responsive. When you are in a professional setting, emotions ought to be buried deep under. This is because creating a habit of becoming emotional in a professional setting will not always have a good implication in your resume. One would rather be calm than emotional because this exhibits that an individual is in a position whereby he or she is able to respond positively to stimuli even in the face of trouble.

## ELICITING CHARISMA

Charisma refers to the personal attributes of an individual, which makes others drawn to them. There are some people whom we find generally attractive, it may not be in their physicality but the manner that they carry themselves. Such people are an aid to be charismatic. The notion with charismatic people is that everybody likes them and owing to this simple fact, they tend to get whatever they want. Charisma entails acting when it is necessary. This means providing a smile where one is due and acting in response with the right emotions t every juncture. Most people fail to notice this but body language goes a mile further when it comes to manipulation. Simple acts like smiling tend to carry huge implications.

When an individual is charismatic, this means that the individual would be able to converse with anyone and make it interesting. Charisma has no limits to age and thus you need to be in a position whereby you are able to pick up a conversation with anyone regardless of the age. One way of making people feel special is through maintaining eye contact. When an individual is conversing with you and you are keen to the extent that your eyes are maintaining contact, you are able to achieve manipulation because this person is visualizing himself or herself as being special. With charisma comes some level of confidence. This confidence refers to the awareness that you ought to first believe in what you are saying before the adverse party can follow suit. You may be talking about the truth or it may be all lies but how you say it will determine how best you are able to manipulate others.

## READING PEOPLE

Human beings are diverse creatures. This is because we have different paths called life. Dependent on an individual's life experience, people have differed psychological and emotional make-up. By this fact, they would thus respond differently to various stimuli that occur. Reading a person will see to it that you are able to push the right pressure points in order to sway the person in your direction. When on the verge of manipulating an individual, one ought to take time and decode the individual's characteristics in order to have an effective plot. Reading an individual will entail that you take note of the various topics that arouse an individual. This means that you are going to take note of the various answers that the individual is going to provide for your questions.

Take note of the emotions of an individual when various topics come up. An individual's emotions are a key pointer to how best you can be able to manipulate the individual. People who tend to exhibit feelings of sadness can be found to be easily bent to breaking down emotionally. Such people would cry just by the sight of a street child, these people are often associated with sympathy votes. They would tend to extend a feeling of empathy whenever you are in a bad situation. When interacting with such individuals, you ought to play in their constraints in order to make sure that they are feeling sorry for you. Once you have achieved this, you are in a position to be able to manipulate them.

To some people, it may be the guilt that is driving them. These types of people may have done something in the past that makes them feel guilty whenever that particular subject is mentioned in the present. They often exhibit a guilt-reflex when that particular subject is mentioned. With this type of people, making them feel guilty is what will enable you to achieve manipulation. Take, for instance, you have an individual who is a past victim of child abuse, this person has been abused as a child and of course, the effects live with him to date. Whenever a topic of child abuse is mentioned, you will find that this individual is responsive and thus making them feel guilty will see you through manipulation.

There are some people, however, who have a logical mind and are able to respond rationally when making decisions. These people are a little subtle when it comes to manipulating them. When you encounter such people, you need to stay devoid of emotions and guilt because they will not respond in a manner that you want. Such people are best manipulated in a calm manner.

# CONCLUSION

At this point, I hope you have gotten a keen insight into the world of dark psychology and all of the aspects that pertain to mental manipulation and and I would like to recommend you the second volume of the series (Speed-Reading People) to learn the art of reading people and how to analyze them. I also trust that you have a newfound appreciation for the way psychology can be used to further your own agenda and plans.

So, what's next?

I would greatly encourage you to take the knowledge you have learned in this book and put it to good use. You can use to fend off those individuals who are looking to take advantage of you while also making good use of the techniques discussed throughout this book for your own benefit.

As I have often pointed out, this book isn't about utilizing people's psyche to rule the world, so to speak. The techniques outlined in this book are intended to help you get the most out of your own talents and abilities by removing barriers which often keep well-intended folks from getting ahead in life.

Ultimately, it is up to you to decide how you will use this information in your own life. But just the fact that you now have a better understand of how others may be trying to influence your opinions and coerce your will is enough to help you get ahead far more easily.

So, do take the time to go over any of the tips, strategies, techniques and concepts contained in this book. By going over the information in this book, you will be able to better fixate the knowledge in your mind.

Also, if you have found this book to useful and informative, do tell your friends, family and colleagues about it. I would greatly appreciate a positive recommendation from my readers.

See you next time.